Pure luck

Sam is bugging me and
I am in a bad mood.

Dad tells me that he has a cure
for a bad mood. It is a fun job.

The fun job is to mix the
soil with the manure.

Then we have to tip it on
to the garden. We moan.

I tell Dad, "This is not a
cure for my bad mood."
Dad winks at Sam and
tells him, "We will see."

Sam and I look down
at the manure.

Sam kicks a hunk of
manure and it hits my leg.

I pick it up and hurl
it back at him.

It hits him on the arm.
He yells and I hoot!
Now that was fun!

Sam thinks that we need to be mature and get on with the job.

I dig into the manure and I
see a bit of foil. No, it is a coin!

I pick it up. Sam
sees a coin too.

We finish the job. We are
hot but we feel good.

Sam yells to Dad, "We are off to the shop. Thanks, Dad!"

Words to blend

bugging	pongs	mood
hoot	that	with
then	soil	foil
coin	garden	arm
moan	winks	hunk
thinks	look	down
hurl	finish	shop

Before reading

Synopsis: Dad gives the boys a job to stop them arguing. They get on with the job and get a nice surprise.

Review graphemes/phonemes: ar or ur ow oi ear air

New grapheme/phoneme: ure

Story discussion: Look at the cover and read the title together. Ask: *What are the boys doing in the cover picture?* (digging in the soil) *Why do you think the story might be called* Pure luck? *Do they look lucky at the moment?*

Link to prior learning: Display the grapheme *ure*. Say: *These three letters are a trigraph – that means they make one sound.* Write or display these words: *pure, cure, mature.* How quickly can children spot the *ure* trigraph and read the words?

Vocabulary check: manure – animal poo that is good for gardens; mature – behaving sensibly, like an adult

Decoding practice: Ask children to flip through the book. See how quickly they can find and read two different words with the trigraph *ure*.

Tricky word practice: Display the word *was* and ask children to circle the tricky part of the word (*a*, which makes an /o/ sound). Practise writing and reading this word.

After reading

Apply learning: Ask: *What are the boys going to do with the coins at the end of the story? How do you know?* (They're going to buy ice creams. We can tell because there are ice creams in their thought bubbles.)

Comprehension

- Who is in a bad mood? Why?
- Were Dan and Sam keen to mix the manure?
- Did Sam know it was Dad who put the coins in the manure?

Fluency

- Pick a page that most of the group read quite easily. Ask them to reread it with pace and expression. Model how to do this if necessary.
- Ask children to turn to page 6 and read the dialogue with expression. Encourage children to consider how Dan is feeling when they read his words.
- Practise reading the words on page 17.

Tricky words review

and	me	he
the	to	we
have	my	of
was	be	into
no	are	for